艺术的传承与升华

Inheritance and Refinement of Art

庞薰琹 丘堤 庞铫 籍虹 庞均

2011

图　录 \ *Inden of Plates*

艺术的传承与升华

庞均

我的父亲谢世二十六年，他留下了六十年坎坷的艺术经验；我的母亲谢世六十三年，她经历了三十余年艺术生涯。战乱与浩劫，只留下很少极珍贵的作品。

他们所留下的作品虽然极少，但其影响力经久不衰，因而倍加珍贵，成为20世纪早年中国现代艺术的代表形象载入史册。对我而言，还有他们那些消失的、大大区别于早年同期留法与留日风格的杰作。他们所呈现的现代美学观、对色线形暨艺术品味之深研，永远成为我们后代创作精神力量的重要部分，这种血脉相传是只可意会不可言传的。父母的艺术活动已成历史，然，在冥冥之中，似乎在西方古典音乐和中国古代文学、诗词之中，仍然可以寻找和感觉到他们的艺术足迹及曾经有过的艺术情怀和理想，所以他们无形的艺术哲学和思想永远活在我们的心田。

以上的时空相隔没有距离。很久以来都想举办一个规模不大但能说明问题的“传承与升华”之学术性艺术展，能够告知天下:“艺术”纯属个人的思想行为，由心而起，非他人（中、外）艺术风格轨迹之照抄与转换。艺术行为源于自然之原创，其表达“语言”之符号，才有可能走向艺术金字塔之顶端。

在精致的北京画院美术馆这个不大的展厅内，把庞薰琹、丘堤、庞铫祖孙的作品并立在七十余年时空距离的空间之中，别具意义。“爷爷”那幅小小的《母与子》，无论色彩、造形、构图、分割、含意都十分现代。“奶奶”那幅参展“决澜社”的作品《葡萄与水果刀》，用笔是那么写意、放松、即兴。孙女庞铫，已有二十年画龄的她，作品完全是抽象、多媒材的当代画风，但她有较深的思考性，有她爷爷、奶奶的灵气，注意构图的装饰感与空间，有文人清雅之画品，黑、白、灰与线条（铁丝与画笔）均能完美地结合。从祖孙的作品相照，可以感受到从近现代艺术演变到当代艺术的内在脉络，并非空穴来风表面求异。

籍虹已有五十年画龄，作品虽然不算多，但凡赏画者，印象颇深。以她自己的话说，要像她婆婆丘堤一样“画少而一鸣惊人”！与其说籍虹喜欢“印象派”，不如说她酷嗜色彩并具有“男性化”的笔触。她曾以爱心饲养过几十只流浪狗、流浪猫，在台湾画坛颇为著名。她对动物之感情与了解极深，刻画动物之灵性亦非同凡响。此外，她爱好画风景与小景，用笔潇洒、结实、厚重，强化人与自然之感情，看似平淡却发人深省。

本人（庞均）有六十余年画龄，自称前三十年只钻研技术（是十分刻苦地研究“印象派”、“野兽派”之技法与理论），后三十年才逐渐精通究竟什么是油画技巧中的“艺术元素”和“美学概念”，从而跨进“表现艺术”的境界，找到自我的表现方式。

学油画必须先西方，后东方，既要“西方”，更要“中国”。前者是精通油画本体的技巧与美学修养，后者是以传统文化作为创作之本，此乃境界与画品之道。单一模仿中国水墨章法以及皴法形态是毫无意义的，中国水墨的笔墨之法与西方油彩用色及笔触肌理等是截然不同的技法，但有异曲同工之妙。

综上所述，本人只追求表现油画色彩、笔触、线条等元素之构成，通过以上抽象元素，传达人性的精神、情感、情绪等抽象思绪与情感，反对教条文化，尊重自然法则，用艺术语言突破中西文化之鸿沟，达到一种崭新的艺术融合。

2011年春季在北京这个画展，倘若对中国艺术产生哪怕是微不足道的学术价值，只要有一点微薄之意义，就是尽了一份文化责任。

我从北京画院走出去，今日又重返北京画院，感觉真好!

艺术路是自已的路。

艺术只能是自然法则。

艺术本是人精神之“私生活”，中得心源。

2011年元旦于台湾

The Passing-on and Elevation of Art

Pang Jiun

26 years ago when my father died, he left behind him 60 years of difficult art experiences; 63 years ago when my mother died, she had experienced a little more than 30 years of art career. Only a few of their works, which are extremely precious, survive the wars and devastation of the age.

Few as their works may be, their influences are enduring and increasingly valuable, as time goes by. Eventually, they migrate to the core of history as representatives of modern Chinese artists in the early 20th century, whose masterpieces, distinct from their early works produced in France and Japan, though have disappeared, remain in my mind. The aesthetics of the time presented in their works, their research into color, line, shape, and artistic tastes, are important imperative for artists of the later generations. This cultural affiliation is unutterable yet substantial. Although the art activities of our parents are gone, their footprints, sentiments and ideals can still be found and felt in the Western classical music and ancient Chinese literature and poetry. In this way, their art philosophy and thinking live forever in our minds.

There does not seem to be any distance between we and they. I have long wanted to hold a moderate-scale academic exhibition on the 'passing-on and discovery' of art, to illuminate the fact that, instead of being a transcription, a transformation, of the styles of others (Chinese or international), 'art' is an act of the mind, a pure expression of one's thoughts; that only the kind of art originating from Nature has a 'language' of signs capable of building up its aesthetic height.

It is exceptionally meaningful to place the works of Pang Xunqin, Qiu Ti, and Pang Yao, distanced from each other for more than 70 years, in the medium-sized yet elegant gallery of Art Museum of Beijing Fine Art Academy. Grandfather's small "Mother and Child" is remarkably modern in terms of either color, shape, composition, segmentation, or connotation. Grandmother's "Grapefruits and Knife," displayed once in the Storm Society exhibition, has an expressionist, relaxed, and improvising atmosphere. Having painted for two decades, Granddaughter Pang Yao's mixed-media works have an abstract, contemporary style, while their inquisitiveness, more persistent than the other contemporary works, are revealing of the spirit of her grandparents. She pays special attention to the decorative and compositional details, and the perfect combination among the colors of black, white, and grey, and lines (made by iron wires and paint brush) reminds one of the dignified, refined tradition of literati painting. From the contrast between grandparents and granddaughter, one can sense the genuine tie between modern art and contemporary art beyond the heterogeneous surfaces.

In her art career spanning 50 years, Chi Hong does not paint much, but her paintings impress none the less. In her own words, she is like her mother-in-law (Qiu Di), who "awed and stunned people with only a few paintings." To say that Chi Hong is impressionist is to downplay her passion for colors and her somewhat 'masculine' style. Besides paintings, she is also noted in Taiwan for having taken in scores of stray dogs and cats. Her deep affection for and understanding of animals are endorsed by the uniqueness of animals shown on her canvas. She also paints landscapes and close views of street corners, of which the neat, sturdy, and thick brushwork works to highlight the connection between human and nature. Seemingly 'plain,' they are thought-provoking.

I (Pang Jiun) have painted for more than 60 years. As I proclaimed, in the former 30 years, I had only succeeded in acquiring techniques (I studied diligently on the techniques and theories of Impressionism and Fauvism); the 'artistic elements' and 'aesthetic concepts' of oil painting had not come to my realization until the latter 30 years. It is only after the 60 years of practice that I am capable of finding the way to expressive myself.

To learn oil painting, you must learn first from the West, before you learn from the East. You have to be Western, but have to be even more Eastern. The former means that you have to be fully acquainted with the techniques and aesthetics of oil painting; the latter implies that you need to base your work on the Eastern cultural tradition, to shed light on the road for you to cultivate the aesthetic character of your paintings. It is simply meaningless to duplicate the rules and strokes of ink painting, which, though congenial with the Western oil painting in some aspects, are drastically different from the latter in terms of color use and brushwork.

To summarize, what I quest for is to master the elements of color, brushwork, and line of oil painting, to express the abstract aspects of humanity such as soul, emotion, and mood. I oppose to dogmatism, and respect the principles of Nature. I aim to bridge the cultural gap between East and West, to attain a new integration by means of the language of art.

If the exhibition held in spring, 2011, have any academic value to the development of Chinese art, however tiny it is, it has fulfilled its cultural responsibility.

Stepped to the world from the gate of Beijing Fine Art Academy, I return to it today. It makes me feel great!

The road of art is a road to one's self.

Art springs only from the course of Nature.

Art is the overflow of one's private life, of one's soul.

New Year's Day, 2011, in Taiwan

母 与 子 *Mother and Child*

纸上水彩 *Watercolor on Paper* \ *36×26cm* \ *1927*年左右于巴黎

C'est le Destin nous fait connaître l'un et
l'autre, ce sera aussi le destin qui nous forcera
prendre chacun leur chemin. Mais ce dessin est
un souvenir de notre amitié et sera toujours.
à Mademoiselle — Jeanette Touchard

海 棠 与 丁 香　*Crabapples and Lilacs*

布面油画　*Oil on Canvas ＼ 65×54cm ＼ 1963*

风雾 *Wind·Fog*

绢本 *Fabric* \ *41×44cm* \ *1947*

唐舞　*Tang Dance*

绢本淡彩　*Oil on Fabric* \ *54×41cm* \ *1946*

苗 女 *Miao Women*

纸本白描 *Line Work on Paper* \ *42×32cm* \ *1944*

唐舞　*Tang Dance*

纸本白描　*Line Work on Paper \ 33×43cm \ 1946*

丘堤
Qiu Di (Schudy)
1906 - 1958

年少在福州女子师范读书时，已突显新女性之特点，带头剪短发，并利用暑期挨家挨户动员家庭主妇学习文化，组织补习班。1928年上海美术专门学校第二届西画系毕业，随后赴日本东京考察学习，受后期印象主义之影响。1931年为上海美专研究员，1932年参加“决澜社”，成为唯一获“决澜社”奖的画家，是中国第一代女油画家。业余爱好是建筑设计与服装设计等。1932年与庞薰琹结为伉俪。抗日战争中，因子女皆幼，忙于家务。1939年利用闲暇时间曾亲自设计、亲手制作百余个布娃娃义卖捐赠。曾绘油画《布娃娃》（现上海美术馆收藏）即是当时之记录。1949年任全国美术工作者协会上海分会委员。1956年为全国美协会员，中央工艺美术研究所研究员。曾为舞蹈演出设计服装，并获奖。1958年3月因心脏病去世。其大量作品因抗日战争及十年浩劫而被毁，现侥幸留世的仅有二十幅油画。上海美术馆收藏一幅双面油画。这批画因奇少而倍加珍贵。

Qiu Di was born 1906 in Fujian province. When she studied at the Teachers' School for Women, she had already begun to act like a new woman in the then-conservative society. She took the lead in having her hair cut short and went door-to-door to convince housewives to learn to read. She even sacrificed her summer vacation to offer them lessons. In 1928, she graduated from the Shanghai Art School with a major in oil painting. After graduation, Qiu Di went to Japan, where she was embraced by the modern art society in Tokyo. Still life was then the main subject of her paintings, which owed much to the Post-impressionist style. In 1932, she joined the Storm Society and became the only artist to win the Society prize. Qiu Di is now recognized as part of the first generation of female oil painters in China.

In 1932, Qiu Di was married to Pang Xunqin. During the War of Resistance against the Japanese, she spent most of her time taking care of their two young children. In her spare time, she was engaged in interior design and fashion design. In 1939, she designed and made by hand more than one hundred dolls for fund raising. They can be seen in her painting 'Doll' (in the Shanghai Museum of Art). In 1949, Qiu Di became a member of the National Association of Artists, and, in 1956, she was appointed a research fellow in the Central Institute of Arts and Crafts. Her custom designs for dance performance won a national award.

She died of heart disease in March 1958. Most of her paintings were unfortunately destroyed in World War II and the Cultural Revolution. Only twenty of them were kept by her family. One of them painted on both sides is in the Shanghai Museum of Art.

静 物 *Still Life*

布面油画 *Oil on Canvas* \ *53×44cm* \ *1931*

决澜社展品 *Entry of Storm Society*

JOHN
MACY

静 物　*Still Life*

布面油画　*Oil on Canvas* \ *37×43.5cm* \ *1928*

决澜社展品　*Entry of Storm Society*

SCHUBY

栀 子 花　*Cape Jasmines*
布面油画　*Oil on Canvas* \ *36×38cm* \ *1941*

根 *The Root*

布面油画 *Oil on Canvas* \ *41×33cm* \ *1947*

堤

厝铫

自 述

庞铫

我关心和热爱的，是绘画能承载人们的情感和传递属于生命的温度。在我的作品里，我用非具象的符号、色块、对象、媒材架构和层迭出一个想象的空间。个人的情感和记忆，经由在创作的过程中和画面的互动而被记录下。理性的平衡一直藏在作品的里层，而感性则作为叙述的手法。

在这几年的展览中，我以时间作为一个线性的主轴，展出三到四年不等的作品。如果单一的作品是呈现了作者当下的某一种视点，那么把不同时间年代，不同尺寸大小，不尽相同叙述方式的作品，以高低错落不规则的方式呈现在一起，形成一定的量体，希望所营造出的视觉语言会是一种时间性的。而在不同的场域和空间中展出，会有不同的作品和排列方式，借此分别出不同量体之间的“消减”或“增生”，就像一个生命体的成长与凋萎。我希望经由呈现方式的不同，让观者看到的不只是很多不同的作品，而是一件具有增减和互动的大型作品。她可以被单独观看，也可被视为某一个部分或时间的片段。让过程和流动的时间填补了作品和作品之间的空隙。

Artist's Statement

Pang Yao

What I care and devote myself to, is the kind of painting bearing human emotions and delivering the temperature of life. In my work, the non-figurative signs, color patches, objects, and media are used to construct and interweave an imaginative space, on which personal feelings and memories are inscribed by my interaction with the elements. While sense and balance are embedded in the texture of the painting, sensitivity is my narrative approach.

Taking the linear time as the axis of my exhibitions in recent years, I exhibited each time works made in a period of 3 to 4 years. If a single work is an expression of the artist's perspective at the time she made it, the body of works, made in different periods, and of different sizes and narrative approaches, when dispersed in an irregular order, will hopefully render a visual language along the temporal dimension. Furthermore, these works, exhibited in different places, by different classifications and ways of arrangement, will manifest a 'reduction' or 'proliferation' among different groups, like the growth and withering of a living body. By presenting my works in different ways, I hope not only to display many different works to the audience, but also introduce them as a large-scale work with the features of reduction, proliferation, and interaction. They can be seen as a single work, as well as fragments of a body or history, among which the interstices are a matter of process and the flow of time.

局部 *Detail*

黑与锁 *Black and Old Lock*

复合媒材 *Mixed media* \ *175×175cm* \ *2006*

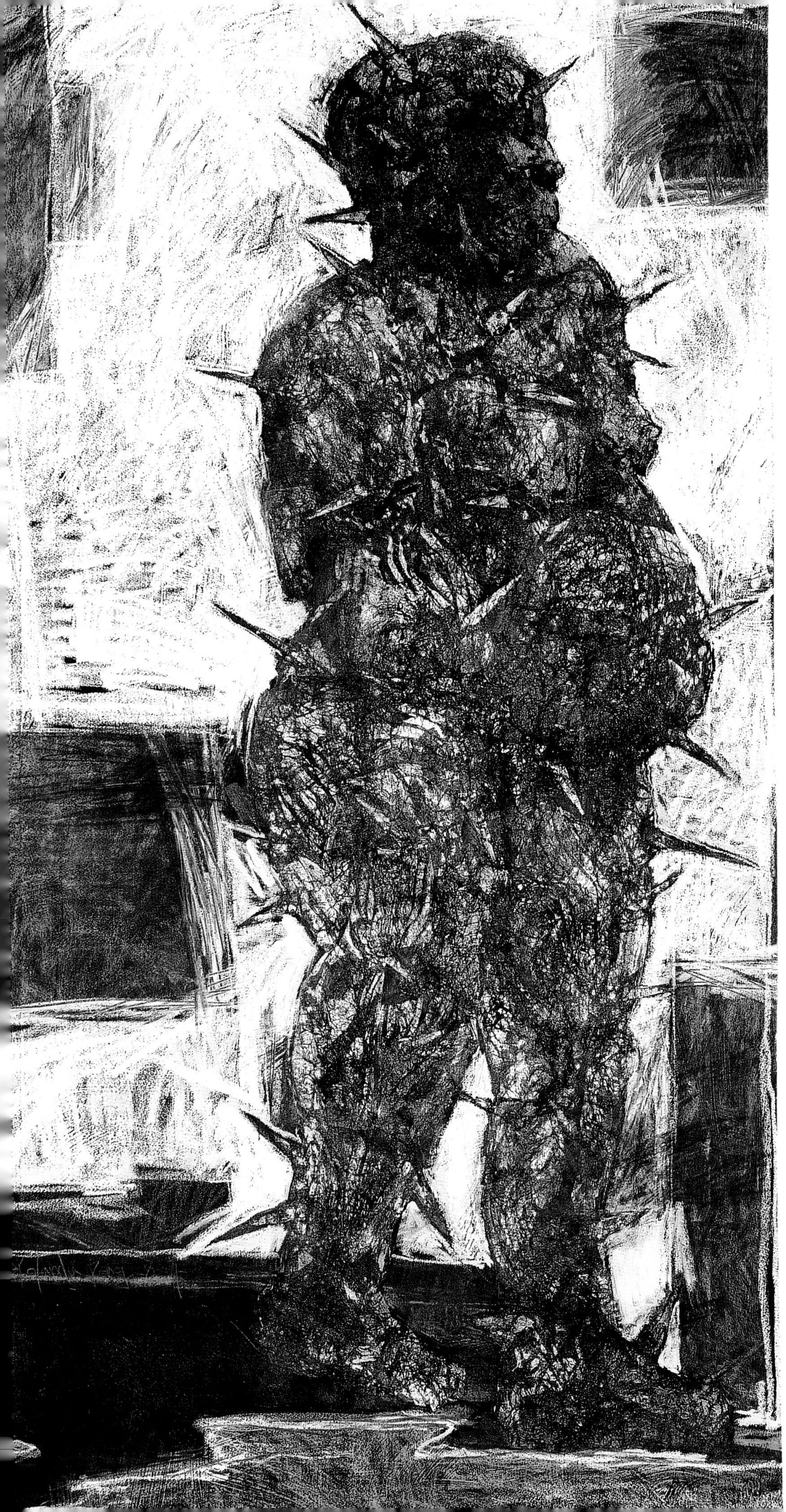

2006漫步NO. 2　*2006Roam No. 2*
玻璃印刷、旧木框、铁
Print on the Glass, Old wood, Steel ＼ 195×86cm＼ 2006

局部 *Detail*

方块与黑 *Square and Black*
复合媒材 *Mixed media* \ *106×106cm* \ *2007*

铁 线 与 白 *Steel Wires and White*
复合媒材 *Mixed media* \ *88×126cm* \ *2007*

灰上的黑十 *Black Cross on Grey*
复合媒材 *Mixed media* \ *68×40cm* \ *2008*

局部 *Detail*

长 角 N O . 1 *Horn No. 1*
复合媒材 *Mixed media* \ *40×68cm* \ *2008*

局部 *Detail*

黑与灰的对话 *Dialogue between Black and Grey*
复合媒材 *Mixed media \ 40×68cm \ 2008*

局部 *Detail*

色块的厚度 NO.2 *The Density of Color No. 2*
复合媒材 *Mixed media* \ *55×88cm* \ *2009*

有 趣 · 无 题 *Tantalizing·Untitled*
复合媒材 *Mixed media* \ *80×40cm* \ *2009*

色　黑色的眼睛 *Black Eyes*

复　复合媒材 *Mixed media \ 40×40cm \ 2009*

局部 *Detail*

缝 *Sew*

复合媒材 *Mixed media* \ *91×73cm* \ *2010*

局部 *Detail*

波 *Splash*

复合媒材 *Mixed media* \ *91×73cm* \ *2010*

局部 *Detail*

色块的想象 *Color Imagination*
复合媒材 *Mixed media* \ 200×230cm \ 2010

小色块 *Small Color Patch*
复合媒材 *Mixed media* \ *40×40cm* \ *2010*

小色块与钉子 *Small Color Patch and Nail*
复合媒材 *Mixed media* \ *40×40cm* \ *2010*

局部 *Detail*

灰色的雾 *Gray Mist*

复合媒材 *Mixed media* \ *72.5×91cm* \ *2011*

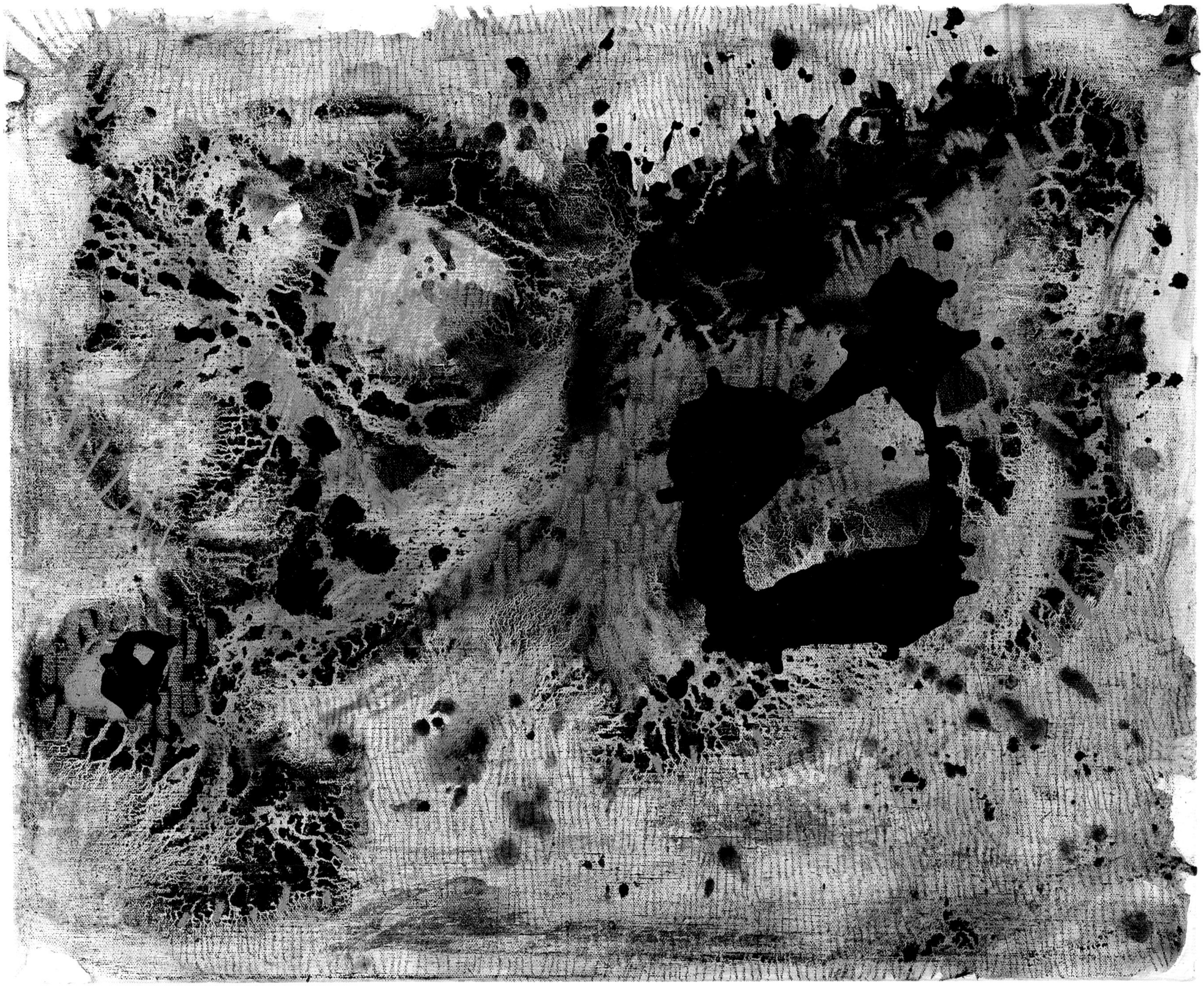

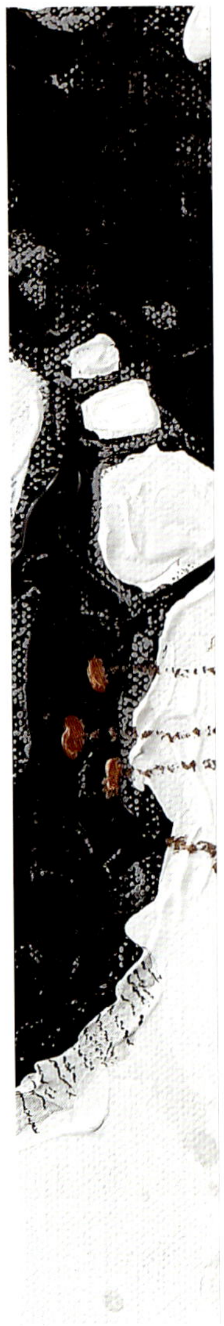

局部 *Detail*

灰色的想象 (

复合媒材 *Mixed m*

84

庞铫简历

1973	生于北京
1980	定居香港
1987	定居台北
1992	私立复兴商工美工科绘画组毕业
	学生美展油画类佳作
	全国美展油画类入选
1995	毕业于国立台湾艺术专科学校（美术科西画组)
1999	获第13届南瀛美展“南瀛奖”（台南县政府文化局）
2000	庞薰琹三代九人艺术展（上海国际艺术节）
	台北县文化节·艺术家大展
2001	个展于台北华艺艺术中心
2002	毕业于美国密苏里州芳邦大学（Fontbonne University)／（艺术硕士 M.A）
2003	北县美术家大展（台北县政府文化局）
	典藏南瀛奖16岁（台南县政府文化局）
	时间的刻度——台湾美术战后五十年作品展（长流美术馆）
	庞氏两代私房画展（新店市立图书馆）
2004	台北县美术家大展（台北县政府文化局）
	毕业于美国密苏里州芳邦大学（Fontbonne University）
	（美术创作硕士 M.F.A）
2006	个展于台中由钜艺术中心（GSR Gallery）
2007	曹筱玥·庞铫（瑶）双姝个展于景文科技大学／万能科技大学
2008	女性艺术创作之美特展——南瀛奖女性得主联展（台南县政府文化处）
	庞铫(瑶) 创作展（绘画与我的距离)，坜新艺术生活馆展出
	9月，上海艺术博览会
	曹筱玥·庞铫双个展于南台科技大学
2008-2009	曹筱玥·庞铫双个展于台中逢甲大学
2009	3月，曹筱玥·庞铫双个展于台中市文化中心动力空间
	4月，曹筱玥·庞铫双个展于龙华科技大学艺文中心
	7月，个展于上海King Space艺术中心
2010	3月，庞铫·林淑婷双个展于台北青山镇会馆
	5月，第二届台北国际当代艺术博览会（YAT）
	7月，个展于上海多伦现代美术馆
	8月，个展于上海King Space艺术中心
	12月，第8届台湾设计博览会
	现任 国立台湾艺术大学、国立台北科技大学兼任讲师

Chronology of Pang Yao

1973 Born in Beijing

1980 Settled in Hong Kong

1987 Settled in Taipei

1992 Graduated from Painting Group, Department of Arts and Craft, Fu-Hsin Trade and Arts School

Oil painting selected by National Students Fine Arts Exhibition

Oil painting selected by National Art Exhibition of the Republic of China

1995 Graduated from Western Painting Group, Department of Fine Arts, National Academy of Arts

1999 Awarded 'Nanying Prize', the 13th Nanying Fine Arts Exhibition, Cultural Affairs Bureau, Tainan County Government

2000 Three Generations of the Pang Xunqin Family, Shanghai International Art Festival

Exhibited at Cultural Festival of Taipei County

2001 Solo Exhibition at Airiti Art Center, Taipei

2002 Graduated with M. A. Degree from Fontbonne University, Missouri, USA

2003 Artists of Taipei County, Cultural Affairs Bureau, Taipei County Government

Sixteen Years of Nanying Prize Collection, Cultural Affairs Bureau, Tainan County Government

The Inscription of Time: Fifty Years of Art in Postwar Taiwan, Chan Liu Art Museum

Selected Works by Two Generation of the Pang Family, Xindian City Library

2004 Artists of Taipei County, Cultural Affairs Bureau, Taipei County Government

Graduated with M. F. A. Degree from Fontbonne University, Missouri, USA

2006 Solo Exhibition at GSR Gallery, Taichung

2007 Works of Tsao Hsiao-yueh and Pang Yao, Jinwen University of Science and Technology and Vanung University

2008 The Beauty of Female Art: Nanying Prize Female Winners Exhibition, Cultural Affairs Bureau, Tainan County Government

Distance between Painting and Me: The Art of Pang Yao, Li Shin Gallery

September Exhibited at Shanghai Art Fair

Works of Tsao Hsiao-yueh and Pang Yao, Southern Taiwan University

2008-2009 Works of Tsao Hsiao-yueh and Pang Yao, Feng Chia University, Taichung

2009 March Works of Tsao Hsiao-yueh and Pang Yao, Cultural Affairs Bureau, Taichung City Government

April Woks of Tsao Hsiao-yueh and Pang Yao, Art Center of Lunghwa University of Science and Technology

July, Solo exhibition at King Space, Shanghai

2010 March Works of Pang Yao and Ling Shu-ting, The Village Club, Taipei County

May Exhibited at the 2nd Young Art Taipei

July Solo exhibition at Shanghai Duolun Museum of Modern Art

August Solo Exhibition at King Space, Shanghai

December Exhibited at the 8th Taiwan Design Expo

Now part-time lecturer at National Taiwan University of Arts, and National Taipei University of Technology

庞铫摄于大茅屋学院

La Grande Chaumière, Photo by Pang Yao

大茅屋学院（La Grande Chaumière）是爷爷庞薰琹（Pang Xunqin）20世纪20年代在巴黎学习绘画的地方。2007年夏天，我和父母造访了巴黎，也找到了大茅屋。就如左侧的照片般，学院只在一楼有一间教室，楼上好像是出租的宿舍。据说现在大多是一些韩国或日本的学生在这里。

当我踏进这教室时，空间中有一种气氛是我喜欢的。我们像是跨越了时空，在一处陌生的环境里却找到了熟悉的感觉。

La Grande Chaumière is where my grandfather Pang Xunqin studied painting in Paris in the 1920s. In summer, 2007, I and my parents visited Paris, and found Le Grande Chaumière there. As shown in the photography left, the academy had only one classroom in the first floor, aside from the dormitory seemed to be for rent upstairs. It is heard that the boarders were mostly Korean or Japanese students today.

When I walked into the classroom, I was welcomed by a favorable atmosphere. Seemed to have transcended time and space, we found at that moment what was dear to us in an alien environment.

籍虹简历

1962	开始学习油画
1980-1987	参加香港年度华人现代艺术展
1989	台北龙门画廊“庞氏家族展”
1991	台北皇冠艺文中心首度个展“花景之情”
1992	高雄三爱创意艺术中心油画个展
1994	台中现代艺术空间油画个展
	被纳入大陆出版《中国当代艺术名人录》
	出版《籍虹油画集》。油画作品广为收藏
	台北亚洲艺术中心“决澜与决澜后艺术现象：庞氏家族联展”
1999	台北县文化中心油画邀请展“为流浪动物表达心声”
	台北县文化中心为籍虹出版《流浪动物油画集》
2000	新店图书馆“籍虹动物油画展”
	高雄文化中心至美轩“籍虹动物油画邀请展”
	多次参加画家联展，作品为广大各国各地收藏家收藏
2006	台中由钜艺术中心“平淡生活中的美”个展
	出版《平淡生活中的美——籍虹油画集》
2007	台北国父纪念馆明德画廊油画个展
2011	北京画院美术馆“艺术的传承与升华：庞氏油画五人展”
	出版合集《艺术的传承与升华》

Chronology of Chi Hung

1962	Studied oil painting
1980 - 1987	'Exhibition of Modern Chinese Artists', Hong Kong
1989	'Pang Family Joint Exhibition', Lung Men Art Gallery, Taipei
1991	First solo exhibition 'For Landscapes with Flowers', Crown Art Center Gallery, Taipei
1992	Solo exhibition of oil paintings, San Ai Creative Art Center, Kaohsiung
1994	Solo exhibition of oil paintings, Modern Art Space, Taichung
	Featured in *Biographies of Contemporary Chinese Artists,* published in Mainland China
	Published Chi Hong's Oil Paintings; oil paintings are widely collected
	'The Art Phenomenon of Storm Society and Post-Storm Society: The Pang Family Joint Exhibition', Asia Art Center, Taipei
1999	'Articulating for Stray Animals', Cultural Affairs Bureau of Taipei County Government, with a catalogue
2000	'Articulating for Stray Animals', Xindian City Public Library
2001	'Articulating for Stray Animals', Chih Mei Hall of Chiang Kai-shek Cultural Center, Kaohsiung
	Exhibited at numerous joint exhibitions; oil paintings are widely collected by collectors of different nationalities
2006	'Beauty in Ordinary Life', Ming De Gallery, National Dr. Sun Yat-sen

Memorial Hall, with a catalogue

2007 Solo exhibition of oil paintings, Ming De Gallery, National Dr. Sun Yat-sen Memorial Hall, Taipei

2011 'Passing-on and Exploration: The Pang Family Oil Paintings', Art Museum of Beijing Fine Art Academy, with a catalogue

2001.

通向海的路（澎湖） *Road to the Sea (Penghu)*
布面油画 *Oil on Canvas* \ *45.5×38cm* \ *2001*

归来 *Return*
布面油画 *Oil on Canvas* \ *38×45.5cm* \ *1995*

在玫瑰城住家常遇此狗
名曰"拿波仑"卡通味十足
无幸得之而画之。

I often met this dog named 'Napolean' at the Rose Town. Having no honor of keeping this cartoon-like dog, I placed him instead on the canvas.

我的邻居拿波仑 *My Neighbor Napoleon*
布面油画 *Oil on Canvas* \ *116.8×91cm* \ *2010*

2010

油菜花 *Cole Flowers*
布面油画 *Oil on Canvas* \ *110×110cm* \ *2010*

看看 *Just Watch*
布面油画 *Oil on Canvas* \ *45.5×38cm* \ *2000*

黑 白 卫 士 *Black Guard and White Guard*
布面油画　*Oil on Canvas* \ *38×45.5cm* \ *2001*

蓝鸟 *Blue Bird*
布面油画 *Oil on Canvas* \ *50×60.6cm* \ *2001*

出游 *Outing*

布面油画 *Oil on Canvas \ 45.5×53cm \ 2000*

KiKi

布面油画 *Oil on Canvas* \ *130×162cm* \ *1999*

小不点 *Little One*
布面油画 *Oil on Canvas* \ *162×130cm* \ *2000*

鸟巢 *Bird's Nest*
布面油画 *Oil on Canvas* \ *65.1×53cm* \ *2010*

2010

妈咪我们爱你 *Mommy We Love You*

布面油画 *Oil on Canvas* ＼ *130×162cm* ＼ *2006*

"有責任心
的麥可"
貪嘴的狗把
頭伸進糧食
袋,麥可便大叫.
小狗們吵架:
麥可就衝到
中間維持秩
序.
羅中立
2000

麦可 *Michael*
布面油画 Oil on Canvas \ *162×130cm* \ *2000*

新朋友 *New Friend*
布面油画 Oil on Canvas \ *38×45.5cm* \ *2000*

台湾农家 *Taiwanese Farmhouse*
布面油画 *Oil on Canvas* \ *35×27.3cm* \ *1997*

台北三峡老街 *Sanshia Old Street, Taipei*
布面油画 *Oil on Canvas* \ *41×32cm* \ *1997*

三步两条桥 *Bridge Three Strides Away*
布面油画 Oil on Canvas \ 65.1×53cm \ 2010

江南人家 *Kangnam Houses*
布面油画 Oil on Canvas \ 65.1×53cm \ 2010

2010

江南街市 *Kangnam Streets*
布面油画 *Oil on Canvas* \ *65.1×53cm* \ *2010*

一品更楼 *Yipin Genglou*
布面油画 *Oil on Canvas* \ *65.1×53cm* \ *2010*

宏村白墙 *A White Wall in Hongcun*
布面油画 *Oil on Canvas* \ *65.1×53cm*

与谌北新大哥对话 *Dialogue with Big Brother Chen Pei-hsin*
布面油画 *Oil on Canvas* \ *110×110cm* \ *2010*

桃花袭人知春暖　*Spring Comes with Peach Blossoms*

布面油画　Oil on Canvas ＼ *65.1×53cm* ＼ *2010*

茶叙　*Tea Time*

布面油画　Oil on Canvas ＼ *65.1×53cm* ＼ *2010*

扶
布

局部 *Detail*

墙头上的咪咪 *MiMi on the Top of the Wall*
布面油画 Oil on Canvas \ *116.8×91cm* \ *2006*

1988年春寒刺骨的風
天，看見賤賣病弱不
堪幼小的大麥丁，十分
可憐！接回家為牠治
病，牠聰明乖巧、伶
俐而後高大，在牠
聰慧憂鬱的眼神
裏我們有過無數溝
通，十年來牠隨我走
過太平山、墾丁、美濃……
……。最終被先天性心
臟病魔帶走了牠，
牠還是那麼乖巧地
默默合上了眼。
嗚呼！哀哉！悲哉！
痛哉！Brambo！
我的101忠狗
享年十歲。
2000 春

蓝波 *Rambo*

布面油画 *Oil on Canvas* \ *130×162cm* \ *2000*

三宝 *Threesome*

布面油画 *Oil on Canvas* \ *110×110cm* \ *2010*

*1966*年坐在邻居抄家的澡盆上拍照　*Photo in 1966*

走！香山写生去！1966年　*Go! To Xiangshan Mountain and Painting! 1966*

庞均简历

1936 出生于上海

1937 开始画油画

1949 进入杭州美术学院

1954 毕业于北京中央美术学院

1956 加入中国美术家协会

1954-1979 专业创作（北京画院等）

1980 定居香港，任教于香港中文大学

1987 定居台湾，台湾艺术大学专任教授

油画各展近40次，理论著作及画册出版十余本

Chronology of Pang Jiun

PANG Jiun

1936 Born in Shanghai

1937 Studied oil painting

1949 Entered Hangzhou Academy of Fine Arts

1954 Graduated from China Central Academy of Fine Arts, Beijing

1956 Joined China Association of Fine Arts

1954-1979 Worked as a professional painter (at Beijing Fine Art Academy, etc.)

1980 Settled in Hong Kong, and taught at the Chinese University of Hong Kong

1987 Settled in Taiwan, and taught full-time at National Taiwan University of Arts

Exhibited for nearly 40 times, and published more than 10 theoretical works and catalogues.

我之所以坚持单一的油画创作六十余年，是为了学习、研究、掌握、贯通西方的油画技术与精神，从而达到超越西方油画的任何表现形式。

The reason that I devote all my efforts to oil painting for more than 60 years is for the sake of studying, researching into, understanding, and mastering the techniques and essence of oil painting, in order to transcend the ways of expression of the Western art genre.

2009

微风吹动了我的头发 *Hair Blown by the Breeze*
布面油画 *Oil on Canvas* \ *175×175cm* \ *2009*

已破烂的庞薰琹出生之楼房 *The Shabby House Where PangXunqin Was Born*
布面油画 *Oil on Canvas* \ *72.7×60.6cm* \ *2010*

莫内花园 *Monet's Garden*
布面油画 *Oil on Canvas* \ *182×452cm* \ *2009*

写意方得笔之力 *Brushwork Fully Displayed in Freehand Style*
布面油画 *Oil on Canvas* \ *60.6×72.7cm* \ *2006*

古镇的水道 *Watercourse in Old Town*
布面油画 *Oil on Canvas* \ *210×301cm* \ *2010*

人体与黑猫 *Human Body and Black Cat*
布面油画 *Oil on Canvas \ 72.7×60.6cm \ 2009*

双 鱼　*Two Fishes*
布面油画　*Oil on Canvas* \ *72.7×91cm* \ *2009*

极端对比 *Stark Contrast*
布面油画 *Oil on Canvas* \ *60.6×72.7cm* \ *2009*

线条 *Lines*

布面油画 *Oil on Canvas* \ *91×72.7cm* \ *2009*

银河轻舟甲天下 *Boats on the Milky Way*
布面油画 *Oil on Canvas \ 194×259cm \ 2007*

黑与蓝 *Black and Blue*
布面油画 *Oil on Canvas* \ *72.7×60.6cm* \ *2010*

500年石板街　*500-Year-Old Street*
布面油画　*Oil on Canvas* \ *60.6×72.7cm* \ *2007*

龙华说法 *Temple*

布面油画 *Oil on Canvas* \ *72.7×60.6cm* \ *2007*

唐朝古镇 *Tang Dynasty Town*
布面油画 *Oil on Canvas* \ *60.6×72.7cm* \ *2006*

剑门石 *Jianmen Cliff*
布面油画 *Oil on Canvas* \ *72.7×60.6cm* \ *2007*

小 镇 商 船　*Barge on the River*
布面油画　*Oil on Canvas* ＼ *60.6×72.7cm* ＼ *2007*

古墙奇石 *Old Wall and Tai Hu Rock*
布面油画 *Oil on Canvas* \ *60.6×72.7cm* \ *2007*

家在琴川　*Qing Chuan, My Hometown*

布面油画　*Oil on Canvas \ 60.6×72.7cm \ 2007*

古镇早市 *Morning Market*
布面油画 Oil on Canvas \ *60.6×72.7cm* \ *2007*

古老的石板街 *Old Stone Slabs Street*
布面油画 Oil on Canvas \ *72.7×60.6cm* \ *2010*

黄色花的魅力 *The Charm of Yellow Flowers*
布面油画 *Oil on Canvas \ 72.7×91cm \ 2010*

种马桥之河 *River under Chung Ma Bridge*
布面油画 *Oil on Canvas \ 72.7×60.6cm \ 2010*

2010

一个休息的姿势 *A Posture of Repose*
布面油画 *Oil on Canvas* \ *80×65cm* \ *1998*

墙外行人，墙内佳人笑 *The Beauty's Laughter on the Other Side of Wall*
布面油画 *Oil on Canvas* \ *200×200cm* \ *2010*

瞬息间的色感 *Color Perceived in an Instant*
布面油画 *Oil on Canvas* \ *60.6×50cm* \ *1994*

向日葵的野性 *The Wildness of Sunflowers*
布面油画 *Oil on Canvas* \ *91×72.7cm* \ *2010*

三步两条桥的老房子 *Old House besides the Bridge Three Strides Away*
布面油画 *Oil on Canvas* \ *72.7×60.6cm* \ *2010*

色彩组合 *The Combination of Colors*
布面油画 *Oil on Canvas* \ *72.7×60.6cm* \ *2010*

PANG JIUN
2010

莲舞 *Dance of Lotuses*

布面油画 *Oil on Canvas* \ *72.7×60.6cm* \ *2010*

黑 背 景 *Black Background*

布面油画 *Oil on Canvas* \ *72.7×91cm* \ *2010*

黑灰与蓝绣球 *Black, Grey and Blue Hydrangeas*
布面油画 *Oil on Canvas* \ *91×72.7cm* \ *2009*

豪门小巷 *Narrow Alley besides a Grand House*
布面油画 *Oil on Canvas* \ *72.7×60.6cm* \ *2010*

2010

灰色之美 *The Beauty of Grey*
布面油画 *Oil on Canvas* \ *60.6×72.7cm* \ *2010*

宏村系列之一 *Hongcun Series I*
布面油画 *Oil on Canvas* \ *72.7×60.6cm* \ *2010*

新年到 *New Year Comes*

布面油画 *Oil on Canvas* \ *91×72.7cm* \ *2010*

一品更楼 *Yipin Genglou*

布面油画 *Oil on Canvas* \ *72.7×60.6cm* \ *2010*

太鲁阁 *Taroko*
布面油画 *Oil on Canvas* \ *72.7×60.6cm* \ *2009*

梅园 *Plum Blossoms*
布面油画 *Oil on Canvas* \ *60.6×72.7cm* \ *2009*

冷色的变化 *The Variation of Cold Colors*
布面油画 *Oil on Canvas* \ *40.9×31.8cm* \ *2006*

鸢尾花 *Irises*

布面油画 *Oil on Canvas* \ *72.7×91cm* \ *2010*

宏村系列之二 *Hongcun Series II*
布面油画 *Oil on Canvas* \ *60.6×72.7cm* \ *2010*

黑红背景 *Black and Red Background*
布面油画 *Oil on Canvas* \ *60.6×72.7cm* \ *2010*

坐赏虞山之美 *The Beauty of Yushan*
布面油画 *Oil on Canvas* \ *53×65.1cm* \ *2010*

戒台寺之松 *Pine Tree in Jietai Temple*
布面油画 *Oil on Canvas* \ *72.7×60.6cm* \ *2010*

2010

巴黎舞者 *Parisian Dancer*

布面油画 *Oil on Canvas* \ *73×61cm* \ *2004*

春桃的舞姿 *The Dance of Peach Blossoms*
布面油画 *Oil on Canvas* \ *130.3×162.2cm* \ *2010*

宏村系列之三 *Hongcun Series III*
布面油画 Oil on Canvas \ *72.7×60.6cm* \ *2010*

黑色背景 *Black Background*
布面油画 Oil on Canvas \ *91×72.7cm* \ *2010*

宏村系列之四 *Hongcun Series IV*

布面油画 *Oil on Canvas* \ *60.6×72.7cm* \ *2010*

色彩构成（百合、玫瑰与线菊）*The Composition of Colors(Lilies, Roses, and Spiraeas)*
布面油画 *Oil on Canvas* \ *72.7×91cm* \ *2010*

2007

对比 *Contrast*

布面油画 *Oil on Canvas* \ *91×72.7cm* \ *2007*

淡雅的灰绿 *The Elegance of Greyish Green*

布面油画 *Oil on Canvas* \ *72.7×91cm* \ *2009*

黄与黑灰 *Yellow and Blackish Grey*
布面油画 *Oil on Canvas* \ *91×72.7cm* \ *2010*

潭柘寺的白皮松 *Lacebark Pine at Tanzhe Temple*
布面油画 *Oil on Canvas* \ *72.7×60.6cm* \ *2010*

千年古松（戒台寺）*1000-Year-Old Pine*
布面油画 *Oil on Canvas* \ *60.6×72.7cm* \ *2010*

极淡的灰色与线条 *Very Light Grey and Lines*
布面油画 *Oil on Canvas* \ *91×72.7cm* \ *2010*

2010

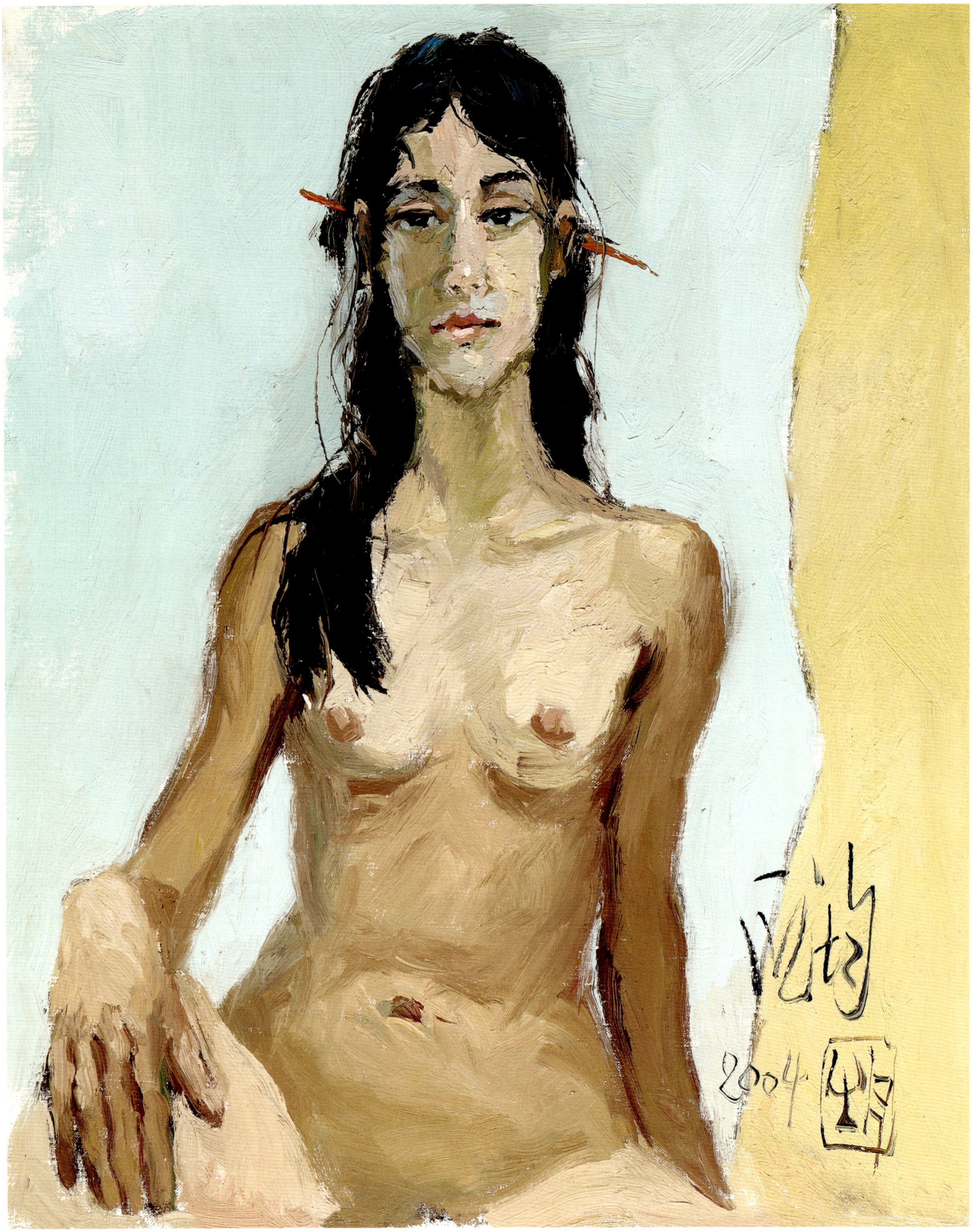

西班牙女子 *Spanish Woman*

布面油画 *Oil on Canvas* \ *65×53cm* \ *2004*

灰蓝之趣 *The Charm of Grey and Blue*

布面油画 *Oil on Canvas* \ *91×72.7cm* \ *2010*

2010

快速的写意 *A Rapid Brushwork*
布面油画 *Oil on Canvas* \ *61×73cm* \ *1998*

窗外春光 *Spring Outside of Window*
布面油画 *Oil on Canvas* \ *72.7×60.6cm* \ *2010*

2010

人人称她大眼妹 *Everyone Calls Her Big-Eyed Girl*
布面油画 *Oil on Canvas* \ *72.7×60.6cm* \ *2010*

黑蓝与紫 *Black, Blue and Purple*
布面油画 *Oil on Canvas* \ *60.6×72.7cm* \ *2009*

2009

MANHATAN
THE SURGE
KUKRI
THE SURGE
2008

兰桂坊 *Lan Kwai Fong*
布面油画 *Oil on Canvas* \ *72.7×60.6cm* \ *2008*

庭院的一角 *A Corner of the Courtyard*
布面油画 *Oil on Canvas* \ *72.7×60.6cm* \ *2010*

随意试笔 *A Freehand Work*

布面油画 *Oil on Canvas* \ *68.5×80cm* \ *1998*

紫色的魅力 *The Charm of Purple*
布面油画 Oil on Canvas \ 72.7×91cm \ 2010

构图　*Composition*
布面油画　*Oil on Canvas* \ *20.8×14.6cm* \ *2009*

苍天无情（小林村的消失）　*God Has No Mercy (The Disappearance of Kobayashi Village)*
布面油画　*Oil on Canvas* \ *175×175cm* \ *2009*

2009

2010

暗红的外套 *The Dark-Red Coat*
布面油画 *Oil on Canvas* \ *72.7×60.6cm* \ *2010*

红、黑、白的构成 *The Composition of Red, Black and White*
布面油画 *Oil on Canvas* \ *72.7×60.6cm* \ *2010*

2010

多色之构成 *The Composition of Multiple Colors*
布面油画 *Oil on Canvas* \ *72.7×60.6cm* \ *2010*

靠卧在黑、白、灰的色彩之中 *Leaning Against the Colors of Black, White and Grey*
布面油画 *Oil on Canvas* \ *73×92cm* \ *2010*

粉色桔梗 *Pink Balloon Flowers*
布面油画 Oil on Canvas \ 91×72.7cm \ 2010

白黑与红紫相遇 *The Encounter between White-Black and Red-Purple*
布面油画 Oil on Canvas \ 72.7×60.6cm \ 2010

12.2010 PANG JIUN

高彩度的组合 *The Combination of High Colors*
布面油画 *Oil on Canvas* \ *91×72.7cm* \ *2010*

红绿与白的构成 *The Composition of Red, Green and White*
布面油画 *Oil on Canvas* \ *72.7×60.6cm* \ *2010*

2010

淡雅的灰绿 *The Elegance of Greyish-Green*
布面油画 *Oil on Canvas* \ *60.6×72.7cm* \ *2010*

多色的组合 *The Combination of Multiple Colors*
布面油画 *Oil on Canvas* \ *72.7×60.6cm* \ *2010*

2010

局部 *Detail*

山 中 有 神 仙　*Mountain with Deity*

布面油画　Oil on Canvas ＼ *300×175cm* ＼ *2010*

冲浪的女性 *A Surfing Girl*
布面油画 *Oil on Canvas* \ *72.7×60.6cm* \ *2010*

设计与绘画 *Design and Painting*
布面油画 *Oil on Canvas* \ *210×210cm* \ *2009*

暗红的背景 *Crimson Background*

布面油画 Oil on Canvas \ *72.7×60.6cm* \ *2010*

局部 *Detail*

2011的第一天（一月一日） *The First Day of 2011 (January 1, 2011)*

布面油画 *Oil on Canvas* \ *195×195cm* \ *2011*

黑底蓝花的裙衣 *Black Dress of Blue Flowers*

布面油画 Oil on Canvas \ *116.8×91cm* \ *2011*

线与色的构成 *Composition of Lines and Colors*

布面油画 *Oil on Canvas* \ *60.6×72.7cm* \ *2011*

黑背景与黄绿 *Yellow and Green in Black Background*

布面油画 *Oil on Canvas* \ *72.7×60.6cm* \ *2011*

鸢尾花的魅力 *The Charm of Irises*

布面油画 *Oil on Canvas* \ *60.6×72.7cm* \ *2011*

蓝色的魅力 *The Charm of Blue*

布面油画 *Oil on Canvas* \ *72.7×60.6cm* \ *2011*

灰紫色调 *Greyish Purple*

布面油画 Oil on Canvas \ 72.7×91cm \ 2011

又是一个春天 *Spring Comes Again*

布面油画 *Oil on Canvas* \ *72.7×60.6cm* \ *2011*

忆MONET花园的花 *In Reminiscence of Flowers in Monet's Garden*

布面油画 Oil on Canvas \ 60.6×72.7cm \ 2011

紫色的温馨 *Cordial Purple*

布面油画 *Oil on Canvas* \ *72.7×60.6cm* \ *2011*

坐看云起时 *A View of Clouds*

布面油画 *Oil on Canvas* \ *175×175cm* \ *2011*

局部 *Detail*

趣在其中 *Thus Lies Pleasure*

布面油画 Oil on Canvas \ 72.7×60.6cm \ 2011

2011

黑与黄 *Black and Yellow*

布面油画 Oil on Canvas \ 72.7×60.6cm \ 2011

此乃趣也 *A Scene of Pleasure*

布面油画 Oil on Canvas \ 175×175cm \ 2011

此乃趣也
2011

我与音乐——论绘画灵感

庞均

事实上，真正好的、境界高的艺术，它的思想性、感情性是融合在艺术的表现力和元素（色彩、造形、线条）之中，而不是简单的主题、题目，更不必强调“重大主题”之词句。原始的人类，就是那么单纯、自然、直接地把思想与情感留在石板与墙壁上，令我们无限感动，只因为它十分真情。

我十一岁至十三岁学习提琴，西方的音符渗透进了我的全部人生之中。对我而言，西方古典音乐调整着我整个绘画心情，激发我的创作灵感。当然我只听那些表现深度很高的音乐家演奏，有很多被大力宣传的演奏“大师”，我甚至听不下去：烂熟的技巧，像背书一样，没有感情。这是一种很神奇的感觉。我想，绘画亦是一样，要想在色彩、笔触、线条中既藏有感情又有文化内涵很不容易。许多修养不是在绘画技巧的范围内可以达到的。故此，我个人认为：油画家（过去称为西画家）完全不懂西方古典音乐，是一种遗憾，甚至是缺陷。中国的诗词也是一种音乐，太有情感了！简练、抽象、激起情感幻觉，这种化学反应，形成了绘画激情和不一样的视觉。

我的每一幅画就是这般地在响亮的音乐旋律中完成。你要问我：这一过程中想些什么？我真的没有想什么，音乐无形地混入色彩之中，线条游走在旋律之中而已。许多作品缺点很多，但并不重要，无意得天趣，有趣、感人就好。七十又五岁，在意何乎？

I and Music – On Inspiration for Painting

Pang Jiun

As a matter of fact, the spiritual and emotional contents of genuinely good and aesthetically exalted art are integrated and embedded into its expressive power and elements (color, figuration, and line), instead of being accounted for by vocabularies such as subject, theme, or even 'motif.' When the primitive people left their thoughts and feelings on the stone slabs and walls, they worked in so simple and natural a way that they moved us with their inherent force.

The musical notes of the classical music have introduced me into the life of all human beings. For me, it is music (the Western classical music) that orchestrates the mood and offers inspiration for my painting, and for certain, I listen only to musicians of expressive depth. Many of the 'maestros' that are trumpeted in the media, their skillful and yet emotionless performances, are indigestible to me. It is a striking fact. I think it is the same with painting, which actually demands tremendous effort to instill emotional and cultural contents into its colors, brushwork, and lines. Cultivation is largely a matter outside of technical concern. In my opinion, therefore, it is a pity, and even a shortcoming, for oil painters ('painters of Western painting,' in the old days) to be totally oblivious to the Western classical music. Chinese verses and poetry are also a kind of music, and one of powerful emotions! Simple, abstract, and emotionally inspiring, the chemistry they generate ignites the passion of painting, and opens up distinctive visions.

Every piece of my paintings is completed in the chiming melody of music. If you ask me, 'What are you thinking when you paint?' I am really not thinking about anything, except that I let the music enter the colors, and lead the movement of the lines. Many of my works may be deficient, but it does not matter. Their merits derive precisely from an unthinking mind, from the pleasure and moving quality they offer. For a 75-years-old man, why take it to heart?

绘画过程不可缺少的伴侣——莫扎特、贝多芬、布拉姆斯、肖邦、布鲁克、帕格尼尼、格拉苏诺夫等谱写的的钢琴提琴协奏曲
Indispensable Companion in Drawing — Piano&Violin Concertos Composed by Mozart, Beethoven, Brahms, Chopin, Broch, Paganini and Glazunov

2010

一个画家对自然界与人类深刻的了解和具有不断写生的能力，是绘画基础之基础。从写生中得到大量经验的积累，逐渐掌控油画本体烂熟的技巧和表现力，这一实践过程与个人灵感、情绪、个性、传统文化精神，化为一体，其最后的表现，无论是写实、写意、抽象、半抽象、复合媒材、构成、观念等，必将升华为真正的艺术境界，成为创造崭新的个人表现形式。因为非凡，必会感动他人。

庞均

2011年1月

It is the basis of basis for a painter to understand nature and human nature thoroughly, and to sketch incessantly. From the accumulation of sketching experiences, the painter is able to learn to grasp the techniques and ways of expression of oil painting, merge them with personal inspiration, mood, character, and cultural tradition, and express them in a brand new, personal style. Whether his\her work is realist, abstract, semi-abstract, mixed-media, constructivist, or conceptual, it must be elevated to an aesthetic height that is extraordinary enough to move people's minds.

Pang Jiun

January, 2011

在巴黎大茅屋工作室作画
庞铫 摄影
Painting at Peinture Académie Sculpture, Paris, Photo by Pang Yao

后记

庞均

此本画册之最后成型，已是2011年的三月间。家庭三代五人展出的作品，因场地所限，作品并不多，因此画册乃是一种补充，具有长期展示之功能。

编辑此本画册的方式颇为特别：每人只负责选出自己的作品与排版，页码无所限制，他人无权过问。故此册之格调如同画品一般，风格各有所异又统一于一册之中。

因为父母之作品数量甚少，国内亦少有所见，故由我代劳编排。

庞铫是要求由她自己在电脑中完成她个人作品的排版设计。虽然她在台湾和美国都没有学过设计专业（Visual Communication Design），但她遗传了她爷爷的因子，很有设计天才，对平面设计和建筑、立体设计很有灵性，颇有感觉和修养。她在台湾电视台Discovery主持“庞铫敲敲门”节目，访谈建筑师维修古屋、装修的新观念等现代设计架构，荣获2010年电视综合节目最佳主持人“金钟奖”，全家对此深感意外。证实优劣自有公断。但她急流勇退，回到自己最爱的艺术创作。近日她在电话中告诉我：“我在研究自己的作品，觉得完全不像你，反而很像爷爷……”我的回答是：“你爷爷的绘画有很浓郁的‘文学性’，你的抽象符号亦重于思考、修养性，不是依赖偶然成形。而我是‘音乐性’，只求色彩对比与灰调的和谐与丰富，重于情绪。在风景中重于中国情怀的诗意性，亦是一种‘文学性’的……”

籍虹之作品由她一人选择排版与写作，表达她的创作动机与理念。她有非常强的个性，无论画画、做事，不容他人干涉，所以她的作品很少有我的意见，往往我认为要补笔之处，她却认为刚刚好。细想之，这恰似她的个性与风格，所以每次当她完成作品，我都只说一个“好”字。她会久久自我陶醉、细品于作品之中……很像自大的印象派画家们。近日她更多地思考如何走向“简单”与“潇洒”。

籍虹颇爱动物，追求生命的意义，虽然历经的坎坷不比他人少，但仍然认为生命是美好的，毫无“玩世”的心态，这在她的作品中表露无遗。她反对丑化动物与人生，为了凸显动物主题，她在画册中大大删减了其他题材作品。在老一代画家中，她唯一佩服的是我的父母，常言：“因为庞薰琹的色彩特别好，才有‘庞均的色彩’。”并自称：“我的作品亦要像丘堤一样‘在垃圾中发现的钻石’。”

在此本画册的最后，我的作品最多。事实上还有更多的作品没有纳入，今年二、三月份还有许多作品颜色未干而弃之入编。以往凡出版或被收藏的作品，我绝不编入新版画册，因为不想老生常谈，过去就是过去了！何以滔滔不绝？然，唯有在大量同时期的新作中，才可感受不同内容与时空色彩之差异及情绪之不同，可谓艺术中有生命之“语言”。由此可见，艺术应有的内涵是不能重复的，不然就是死去的灵魂。

有人说：“庞均画画太快”，此言差矣！贬意实不公平。六十多年来，我的两块调色盘颜色从未干过。目前已经“退休”数个调色盘，作为不花钱的“装饰品”挂在画室内，本人亦站立作画六十余年。我早就放弃了学院“课堂习作”追求精准技术的画法，走向了自我感觉与追求情感元素的表现方式，故此强迫自己作画一笔不改，一气呵成。这一切都是为了追求中国传统“气韵生动”和“意境”的艺术哲学，为此我付出了极大的苦功。

我的艺术生活与创作活动，无时不刻是在响亮的西方古典音乐声中。年复一年地生活就是如此……习惯了！自得其乐。

艺术必定不是虚构地、说明性地矫揉造作、哗众取宠之物。艺术应有它扎实的文化内涵和美学与学术价值。

2011年3月

Afterword

Pang Jiun

In March, 2011, this catalogue is finally brought to completion. Because of a limited space, the exhibition can only display a certain number of the works of the five members, three generations of the Pang family. The catalogue is therefore a supplement that functions as a location of permanent exhibition.

The editing of this catalogue is extraordinary: everyone is supposed to be responsible for the selection and layout of the images of his or her own works. There is no limit to the number of pages, and no one has the right to question the others' decision. This catalogue is therefore a collection of styles, which are heterogeneous and yet harmonious.

And because there are few materials about my parents, and some of them have appeared in other publications, I took the responsibility of the layout of their images on their behalf.

Pang Yao had requested to design the layout for her works on her own computer. Although she was never trained in visual communication design, she has inherited the genes from her grandfather. Her instinct displayed in the fields of graphic design, architectural design, and three-dimensional design has a logic and depth of its own. She was the host of the program 'Pang Yao Knocking at the Door' on TLC Channel. Fir it, she had interviewed the architects for their projects of conserving ancient buildings and concepts of modern design, which won her the 2010 Golden Bell Award for the Best Host in a Comprehensive Programme, to the surprise of the family. It is a sure proof of the existence of an inherent principle of good and bad. However, she decided to put aside the achievement to return to her favorite work: art. She told me recently, 'I am analyzing my own works these days, and I feel that they have more affiliation with Grandfather than with you...' I replied, 'Contrary to your grandfather's paintings, which are suffused with a "literary" atmosphere, and the abstract signs on your canvas, which are guided by thoughts and spiritual cultivation, and independent from fortuitousness, my paintings are 'musical,' in the sense that they quest solely for the harmony and affluence of the contrast of colors and grey levels, for the expression of moods. To landscapes, they center on the poetic sentiment in the Chinese tradition. In this sense, they are also 'literary'..."

The layout of Chi Hong's works and words are also chosen by herself to express her motives and ideas. Having a strong character, she never allows people to interfere with her work or daily affairs, and my comments on her paintings are no exception. To my suggestions of adding strokes, her usual reaction, true to her character and style, is to ponder on it for a long time, before any action is taken. As a result, whenever she completed a painting, the only word I said is "Good," and then she would be complacent with her own performance, much as a Impressionist painter is complacent with his works... Recently, her attention is placed on a 'simpler' and 'more unrestrained' expression.

Chi Hong loves animals, and is intent on exploring the meaning of life. Although she had suffered much in the past days, she never adopts a hedonistic view of life; rather, she lays eyes on the bright side of life, which is the constant theme of her paintings. Refusing to besmirch animals and life, she removed many images of paintings with subjects other than animals in this catalogue. The only painters of the older generation she admires are my parents. She often said, 'It is thanks to Pang Xunqin's excellent command of colors that "Pang Jiun's colors" are notable.' About her paintings, she added, 'My works, meanwhile, will take the example of Qiu Di, to "discover diamonds in garbage".'

The latter part, and also the larger part, of the catalogue are composed of my works. In fact, in addition to the paintings I made in February and March, of which the paint has not dried yet, a large number of my works, including those in the collections or whose images were published, are left out of the catalogue. What is past is past; what is the point of repeating myself endlessly? It is in the new works made at about the same time that one can perceive the differences in content, colors, and moods, that is, the 'language' of life in art. Accordingly, the repeated content of works denotes the death of soul.

The comments that "Pang Jiun paints too fast" are far from the truth. Their pejorative meaning is not only unjust, but also rashly made. For more than 60 years, two of my palettes have not dried, and the other palettes already 'retired' are hung on the wall of my studio as costless 'decorations.' Having standing before the easel for more than 60 years, I have long renounced the academic 'studies' demanding precision, and moved towards the expression of feelings and emotional elements. I force myself, consequently, to complete painting at a stroke, in hope of achieving the 'lively aura' and 'spiritual state' as described by the Chinese art philosophy. My efforts at this task are tremendous.

Every instant of my art life, every fruit of my creative activities, is fulfilled in the chiming notes of the Western classical music. My life has been like this for years... I am used to it, and to the pleasures it offers to me.

Art is not fabricated for the purposes of 'make explications' and arousing sensation; rather, a work is qualified as art only when it has intrinsic cultural content, aesthetic value, and academic significance of its own.

March, 2011

图书在版编目（CIP）数据

艺术的传承与升华 / 庞均著. ——北京：文化艺术出版社，2011.4
ISBN 978-7-5039-5022-3

Ⅰ. ①艺… Ⅱ. ①庞… Ⅲ. ①中国画—作品集—中国—现代 Ⅳ. ①J222.7

中国版本图书馆CIP数据核字(2011)第048278号

艺术的传承与升华

作　　者：庞薰琹（1906 - 1985）丘堤（1906 - 1958）庞均 籍虹 庞铫	Author: Pang Xunqin, Qiu Di, Pang Jiun, Chi Hong, Pang Yao
摄　　影：林裕翔	Photograph: Lan Yushyang
责任编辑：吴士新	Edition Editor: Wu Shixin
设　　计：雅昌设计中心	Design: Artron Design Center
出版发行：文化艺术出版社	Published by: Culture and Art Publishing House
地　　址：北京市东城区东四八条52号（100700）	Adress: 52, Dongsi 8 Alley, dongcheng district,beijing(100700)
网　　址：http://www. whyscbs.com	Website: http://www. whyscbs.com
电子邮箱：whysbooks@263.net	E-mail: whysbooks@263.net
电　　话：(010)84057666 84057660（总编室）	Telephone: (010)84057666 84057660(Editor-in-chief Office)
(010)84057690 - 84057699 64813386（发行部）	(010)84057690 - 84057699 64813386(Publish Dept.)
经　　销：新华书店	Sale: Xinhua Bookstore
印　　刷：北京雅昌彩色印刷有限公司	Printed by: Beijing Artron Color Printing Co., Ltd.
版　　次：2011年4月第1版	Publishing Date: First Edition In April, 2011
2011年4月第1次印刷	First Published In April, 2011
开　　本：889×1194mm 1/12	Product Dimensions: 889×1194mm 1/12
印　　张：25	Printed Sheet:25
书　　号：ISBN 978-7-5039-5022-3	ISBN 978-7-5039-5022-3
定　　价：380.00元	Price: RMB 380.00